A HEART AND MIND DIVIDED

selected poems
1977 - 2006

Jody M. Lewis

selected paintings and graphics
1978 - 2000

Marilyn D. Brown

for Randi,
who reads and understands
from a nearby peaceable path

ISBN 0-9772115-2-5

Printed in the United States by
Independent Publishing Corporation
St. Louis, Missouri

http://www.whitecanoeproductions.com

Contents

ART PLATES

I.   **Traveling Toward the Light - acrylic on paper**
     Ladies in Waiting - acrylic and pastel on papers

II. **The Dream Pillow - acrylic and oil stick on papers**

III. **Angels at the Table - acrylic and pastel on plexiglass**

IV. **Hearthquake - acrylic, pastels on paper**
     Cinderella Fleeing - acrylic, pastels on papers

V.   **The Monk - acrylic, pastel on paper**
     Passing of the Elders - acrylic and ink on paper and
     acetate

VI. **The Ice Village - acrylic on paper**
     Fragile Boxes - acrylic on papers

VII. **The Geyser - acrylic on paper**
     A House Divided - acrylic and pastels on paper and
     plexiglass

VIII. **In a Ghostly Sculpture Garden - computer graphic**
      using Bryce 3-D software
      Aragorn - computer fractal plus drawing

A preface from the heart. . .

These poems may reach out and speak to some while turning others away. They are personal and, possibly, more comfortable for kindred spirits and less so for those who see life another way. All, though, may recognize the feelings that are the heart of the book: idealistic hopes, frustration, grief, anger, and renewed hope, reclaimed optimism. These are cyclical reactions, not permanent states; therefore, I made the decision not to put the poems in their chronological order.

For as long as I can remember, I have been torn between heart and mind, feeling and thinking. They are rivals for my trust and my belief. I recall learning the beautiful word "mystic" when I was about eight years old and setting my own inner goal to have a life of mystical intensity to whatever degree I was capable. It is, in our society, relatively unusual, but that is the kind of life that has always drawn me; and in turn I have tried to portray it in words and to share it as well in images.

A preface from the mind. . .

How does the rational mind deal with spiritual encounters? That is the essential question that occupies my daily life. It is not that mind revels in denying its experiences; it is that it is too often stopped cold by its need for logical explanation. The dream world has a logic of its own, but its rationality may not survive in the waking world. While heart may thrive in the inner life, mind has to function in the external life as well. My goal is to merge the two and find no contradiction, but accomplishing that goal has become a major challenge.

Whether you are a kindred spirit or a visitor to alien land, welcome to my seesaw world.

Jody M. Lewis, 2006

A Heart and Mind Divided

Old dreams wait cluttered
in veins of older rock.
I cart their many fragments to the surface
where they acquire wings,
but some days only silence sings.

Up from shadowed mines
like ghosts from cave-ins past,
these gray canaries fly,
dissolving slowly against the grayer sky.
I send them off to jolt the hills,
collide with what is set in stone and dust,
and return to me, as return they must.

It's hard to trust.
My mind prefers to fill
with that which never will run dry,
with what will last;
but heart entwines
itself among beloved things.
It clings to textured surface
while mind forever wants to knock
on dreams' deceptive plainer doors
to find words long unuttered
and be let in on truth.

Evening by the Springs

What hisses and scares
in the darkening grass
and in the ominous basins of heat?
Phantoms, nothing.

We watch from a distance,
the children and I,
the clouds of steam that rise from the vents
and churn from the mud-boiling springs.

Dark thoughts trace the trail with me,
curling through patches and remnants of fear
embroidered with wonder.
I seem to sense at each new turn
pale rough unknowns, slim spectres,
enlarged by inexperience.
We hurry slowly toward the steam's source,
eager to see, reluctant to find.

Near the less rapidly bubbling sinks
and craters crusted with lime,
tiny birds test the water's thin edge,
skitter away, and return.
Softly I take my children's hands
for the swift comfort of their warm flesh
and of their trustingness.
Together we pass the shadowing spots
beneath the branches where insects hum
and where white fragile webs entrap
the last pale light.
Together we move like the smallest birds
toward new excursions tentatively;
and I am stretched by my ambivalence
to want to reach for my own sake
no less than that of my children's,

while wanting, too, to be caught in the steam,
held like the light in the web,
indifferent to the pulsing in the dark grass,
unaware of the gathering sundown.

You There

Nameless to me the constellations,
though I have studied
through the wakeful hours
their moving forms.
You sleep so still
through each protracted dark–
an inert shape, a body, a name–
and yet a constellation
by whose configuration I am puzzled,
by whose detachment I am left alone.

So I turn dreamless to the cornered stars
as if they offer more than you
simply because they radiate light,
moving presences however remote.
I would rather move you
to brighten us, to circle you closer to me,
to puzzle you out of your steady path
that leaves me here in the dark.

I would shower you with meteors,
shoot you with stars,
but you sleep so still–
a body, a name.

Mismatch

She does not understand:
he waters the grass
in the midst of rain
and eats at preselected times.
He reads until it is time to stop

whether he wants to read
or stop
or not.

He hides in schedules,
timetables of an ordered life,
drummers of his days.

He does not understand:
she forgets that plants needs watering,
assuming they fend for themselves,
having survived for eons without her.
She eats on a tide of emotions.
She dreams until it is time to stop
and goes on dreaming in spite of time.

She hides from schedules,
timetables of a robot life,
mechanical drummers.

Wizards Came Calling

Wizards came calling; their voices
altered the light and fired the evening sun.
Smoke hung in the air in August
and soft green leaves thought they were done
and fell to earth, pale acts that called for mourning.
I knew then it was time to move, to find the hills,
the shaded spots, the deeper green
in which a heart rejoices when summer,
too oppressive, leads to dust and pain.

Walking was harder then, breathing more an effort;
but something called, reminding me of forest paths
and solitude and simple spells.
(Merlin, was yours among the voices?
Come out from your hooded shadows.)

They said that cold would come that fall
before October; snow in September might last
clear through to March.
Great trees might break beneath the sleet and ice,
and fragile birds might freeze before they ever flew.
And it was so.
I asked myself through all the bleakest time
if I would hide again from cold,
fold in coddled from winter,
nestle in comforts of down, refuse to test the sky
because of unknown voices.

Or are these speakers who surround me here,
I asked, echoes of deep healing come to call?
Would their wings uphold me
through driving snow?
their voices linger as a beacon to the way?
or doubts assail me as every shadow loomed?
How could I know?

All signs are ambiguous,
all omens from the Sphinx,
who cares not if we understand.
Her task is simple: to present,
ours to bend our minds to comprehend
or not.
The inks with which our maps are written
run in snow and sleet,
are not made visible by heat
or even light.
Our compass points go spinning.
The beat to which we march year-round

falters and fades to an old routine.
We cannot count on messages
we find outside ourselves.

Goodbye, oracles. Only one may stay.
Merlin, my spirit-bitten bard,
my patron saint, be silent now beside me
and let me learn to recognize *my* voice, *my* song.
However hard it prove to be,
however long I'm doomed to take,
whatever help I ask along the way, even now,
be silent for my sake
until I come back home.
Then welcome me.

On that day all your friends and mine may call
at open gate, at unlocked door,
float in the air as long before,
display their deeper magic,
bringing life from chaff.
Leaves will rise dancing from the forest floor;
and I will smile, sing,
laugh.

Promise, Omen

I wore a mask of competence;
all things seemed fit.
Good comes, I thought, to those strong souls
who stand and wait collected
behind their funny faces.
I would be one of them.
Was that a promise?

Privately the mask fell;

good floated past or wrinkled overhead,
skittered to corners if it existed at all.
Strife grew in brand new places.
Nothing fit.
Was that an omen?

Outdoors, chain saws around the town
were buzzing dead trees down,
roaring through imminent woods
where I could hear the fall and crash.
What braces keep us standing tall,
safe from the lash of evil?
Too often none at all. . .
and so I opened windows to let the sounds
and let the scent of sawdust come flowing in,
but the saws were razing summer.
Would masks fall too? and need of them?
It seemed a promise.

Where were the rabbits that always had nibbled
the grass in the fields?
Fewer in number and thinner than ever,
they'd slipped through the fences and vanished
as wild returned.
Here in the civilized suburbs
rabid raccoons came striking,
foraging deep in the night.
It seemed an omen.

Eons passed or days.
Then months, years, filled with everpresent pain
and timeless grief, and all my tears did nothing
but hollow me like those dead trees
awaiting chain saws, breathing dust.
What could change and what could I do? what be?
what see? Would I go on hiding?
These were ominous questions.

Tears went dry, leaving only prayer
there on symbolic knees.
"Show me my life, not yet my death."

Slowly, slowly, plump bunnies fed on green grass;
raccoons returned to woody nests in those
same hollow trees. Saplings rose,
so promising an image.

I'm learning truth may come to those
who cannot wait collected;
who raze themselves since nothing fits;
who wildly want to slip away
to truer love– rushing fences, vanishing,
leaving masks behind them.
Some force will sometimes intervene
to open eyes, to make old symbols new.
It drops a filmy vision, suggests a hazy path.
In words, in wood, in paint, in stone,
in dreams it makes its presence known.
Some drive to life incarnates as a phantom voice
and phantom breath; it comes to whisper,
ambiguous to me:

*"Now art thou free!
I bring an omen ripe with promise
if thou be thee."*

My Merlin Cave

It is silent here, for I work best that way.
It is not cold, for I have tapestries of blue
with strands of copper weaving through;
and here and there are threads of ivory and white
reminding me of old times.

No closets,
for I have little need of things.
I store a bag or two of food
and tea to brew: blackberry
for when I'm in a quiet mood
and orange spice as my reward
when life in caves gets hard.

I've pasted bronze-eyed angels on the walls,
and saints of my creation hover near;
no little creatures scurry in the corners,
but gods of my imagining are here.

No locks.
No magic of an ordinary kind;
no apparitions, voices, spooks from inner worlds–
but dreams that lure me into presences
that merely speak of glory in the mind.

No promises that I'll stay here forever;
no covenants like rainbows on the stones;
and yet no life I've witnessed in abundance
can claim my love or offer more
or recreate my spirit more
than what I find in this blue cave,
mining copper dreams of angels,
carving ivory saints from my pale bones.

Cycling

I kept cycling toward beginnings,
wheeling roadless into blue,
higher than the pleated clouds
that crown the distant ridges
until he'd spring his fears on me
and I'd then spiral down.

I counted scattered crimson flowers
weaving through the matted green,
but he'd tell me it was blood
that I had never seen
correctly.
Back to the start I'd go,
driven by his losses.

Then it was crimson silence,
not a flower anywhere
nor a burst of autumn sunshine
on the muddy road he'd mapped.
He'd want us wrapped together
in his narrow halls.
He sent me cycling toward all endings,
pedaling footless in the snow;
and because I did not know who was right,
if anyone was right,
I finally let go.

Now many years have flown
but again I cycle toward beginnings.
I still wheel upward, scanning the clouds
for a place to peer through,
to get a glimpse of what's beyond
those ragged shrouds of white.
I look for mirrors in the high still air,
fond of the thought of purpose,
though my mind denies.
Something within cries out for answers
and something external sometimes replies,
telling me the flowers are not blood
nor is the road all mud,
and the tree is more than wood
for it blossoms in its season
when it should.

I Dream of a King, a Pitcher, and a Knight

He is a stoic king, staring straight ahead,
evincing not a clue that he has feelings.
His stern sword lies across his royal lap,
awaiting his pleasure,
if he has one.

Sedately a knight enters from the right,
comes before the throne kneeling.
His own broken sword signals his submission
to his liege; his visor is gone,
though he had one.

A liveried footman brings in a platter
on which is sitting a pitcher. Up at the ceiling
birdwings flutter, whispering commotion,
while below in a steady and deliberate measure
the king rises up to his task.

He smites the pitcher, slicing it in two,
but both halves remain intact, standing.
Blue water falls in a bowl like treasure
and the knight is unable to ask
what he would.

Again the sword rises and descends like light,
and the knight collapses in two, still breathing.
One repressed shudder, a single seizure,
and the king begins to bask in the good
he knows he has done. He even smiles.

Birdwings flap and flutter and rustle.
There is a moment of ice, then silence.
Who will render accounts for this Caesar?
But there is no need,

for see what he has done:

in the flutter of a wing,
all things he has transformed;
nothing is as it was.
The king stands tall, half a king and half a pitcher,
pouring out his love upon all people.

The knight stands tall, half a knight and half a king,
for where is power vested?

The pitcher of love– or is it wisdom?–
half a pitcher, half a knight–
flows now with a loyal heart.
All sit down on the throne they now must share,
basking in the good that they have done.

The choir of birds intones a solitary note,
all of them singing as one.

A Kind of Thanksgiving

Gray-brown are the simple weeds
that line the edge of the creek;
black is the bark of the winter trees;
black are the withered berries.
Darkly the brittle, fragile stems
and grumbled bark and clotted berries
stand against the whitened rocks
and little pockets creekside,
dusted after snowfall.

It is a silent, starkly cleansing scene
that finds an echo behind my eyes

at the cusp of thinking.
The air is motionless and cold,
befitting winter's deadly settling in.
Somehow the day has finally come to this,
a quiet walk in the gray dusk
as lights are slowly blinking on
down here on Earth
and in the dark beyond.
It is not a time for bold deeds,
nor time to plan the complex week.
It is a time to give the mind a little ease,
relief from day's strife and midnight's worries.
It is a time to take a deep breath of cold air
and be glad of suspended moments.

Gray Time in My Mother's Day

Sometimes the night comes softly
to her deaf ears.
The blanket does not even wrinkle,
and no ghost appears.
She wonders why
and asks with a tearless sigh
and in words not all that clear
when is her turn?

Daylight is the foe
when it comes with pain.
She naps through countless hours,
trying to become a ghost again.
She has forsaken all tasks but this:
to die well loved, suspecting it might not be so.
She asks if I will miss her,
thinks that others want her gone.

Yes, I'll miss you, I say. She smiles,
but does she smile to say she's glad
or does she think she's caught me in a lie?
She does not know for sure,
nor do I.

She calls me *mother* when wanting earthly care,
calls *Mother, Mother,* for a different kind of care.

Sometimes death's wolf comes howling,
and the moon glows near.
She feels the cold approaching,
but she has no fear,
Her eyes almost twinkle;
a smile will crinkle the pale cheek,
but the wolf lopes by.
Death, she feels, is taunting her;
relief and disappointment mingle in her mind,
pale imaginary dancers
who weave their way into her dreams
and in the midst of their performance
disappear.

Near the Tree Line

I traveled west, escaping flatlands
and hiked with unaccustomed breaths
toward all that blue above
like a glorious alcove, a canopy of sky,
incapable of death.

Near the tree line, the effects of altitude
come into view: pines are askew,
their thin stands twisted anew

to gnomish shapes,
Only the little forms of life
scoot and scurry in the barren cracks;
the mountain jays are at home,
and the chipmunks frolic.
Here is literal life at the edge.
It is a visual trick,
for the grass is sparse and disappearing,
totally absent a short way up.
The bursts of wildflowers,
sparkling the slopes a few steps down
are fast receding,
the thin air impeding
all thought of growth.
Wind and rain and ice
have carved each crevice;
avalanches have tried to bring the mountain down.

It all looks straightforward, though it is not.
Appearing to defy confusion,
its message clearly demands we choose
life or death,
but it is indifferent to the answer.

I cannot climb;
I am no battler of these huge forces
time has created here;
my mind freezes at every menace
lurking in every step.
I falter at the thought
of a single misplaced foot.
But here at the tree line where life divides
and offers directions in symbolic ways,
I'd choose the rock with its deep clefts,
its bare peaks, its cold beauty in the thin air
and in its folded strength
enduring for days beyond human number,

seeming immortal– outliving grass, outliving wood.
I'd choose it if I could.

I end my weak attempt to reach heaven.
I return to the car, having come this far
and unable to go farther.
I have inscribed my human limits.
Unable to rise to the rock's true challenge,
I will rest in its mighty illusions.

Beached

It was summer, and I waited
for the rising waves to reach
me where I stood and
surge me with their power
to the gray sand beach.
I never grew accustomed
to the footing or the motion
of the sands shifting from beneath me
and tumbling toward the ocean
in a dizzy sort of way.

I watched the slim gulls gliding,
scavenging for fare,
gracefully riding
upward curves of air
and landing.

Summer winged the gulls
to their own sure footing
on the slanty shores.
Summer dulled urgency,
reduced the gulls to casual looting

where the beaches were overfull.
No great needs in summer.

Landlocked, though, in winter,
we sense a different rising power
that threatens to engulf us where we stand,
carrying us nowhere
and letting even old familiar footings strand
us in the middle of confusion.

We need a wider wingspan to balance us,
need a broader base than human feet provide.
We want to soar above the shifting sands
and rise above the highest tide
and look about
and see the truths
that bring life's oceans down to our own size.

We need to stand on towering peaks
and see the world with more than human eyes.

Near to the Dark Again

What does it matter that the world is green
and the bright sphere spins
in a wondrous race,
that every richly complex scene
before me wins
its own most holy place
if I grow small in the fierce embrace
of driving needs
and tense ambition
and in tight corners I erase
my recent gains and recent deeds

and new precision
in finding and describing space
where once-invisible spirits gleam?

If I again go wandering lost,
then what does it matter
if a mighty host
of angels dance in every beam,
if, blind, I cannot see them chase
the stars and suns around the sky?

Awaiting News That Never Comes

On these December days
words of green must wrap me
like a tree wooled out with leaves.
Small tracks across the quilted snow
must comfort those sharp moments
when nothing in the day's events
embroiders life or weaves
new patterns in.

No news arrives.
The hours unravel; the day frays;
work yields no delight;
and all the starry skies of night
are just a blurry darkness
or a haze of spotted white.

I'd like to build a fence
of sleep around these times–
enter when I please
and dream the time away.
For then I'd slow the day's pace down
and bring a temporary peace

that lets both mind and heart release
the toxins of these frantic days
when every muscle's tense
awaiting news that never comes
to simplify our lives.

Touch

I touch you;
are you there?
Disguised behind a wall of words
as equally in silence,
you obscure self
in a haze of gray abstractions
so that I may not reach you.

You touch me
and I sense that we are both alone,
lost in our separate shells of self
that open on separate shores.
Disguised within my images
that often seep to silence,
I seem to hide from you more deeply
in every concrete act
so that you cannot hurt me.

Understatement

help, help,
in a muffled voice
I called unimaged

and in no drastic words,
for all of me was understated,
less than I could be
or hope to see
expressed.
Well, was my voice then
so unreal that you could turn
and even smile?
out, out,
in a whisper I demanded toneless
and with no attempted
show of force or strength,
for I was without doors
by which to make my exit.
Then was my need
so insignificant
that you could turn some key of self
to off
and walk away, just disappear,
untouched?

Free now,
in a quiet voice
and a whisper undemanding
that finds no need
of drastic words
nor images that reek of violence,
I find my voice is suited to myself
and I am free to turn
toward what I will:
toward God, toward self,
toward all that draws me to it.

Yet, I still pause by choice to ask you now,
Is this new freedom I now find
significant in realms of yours,
real enough beyond myself,

that you will turn and share it
in all its varied images
keyed to varied doors?

Moving Strangely On

It's spring almost,
mild enough now to get right out
to walk the warmer weather route
I followed years ago.
Once more the scraping sounds of neighbors
cleaning out dead leaves and raking thatch,
washing windows, moving heaps of trash,
aggressively snatching these milder days
for all their labors,
beset my ears.

I am no match for them, but
this year I'm feeling that I know
wherein there's hope for me
and where there's none.
This year I don't expect
to be confronted by a rake
or mop or broom or dusting rag.
I don't anticipate a scene
in which the measure of this year's dust
is noted on eternal scrolls
or kept beneath some heavenly rug
to trip me up on wrinkles.
By now I am aware
that my own act of cleaning up
takes place within invisible rooms,
that as I rearrange myself
and find Me in the dustless, spotless places,
the sight of all that visible work of others
nags at me no more.

No one here is keeping score.
It's spring almost
and time already
to climb the trees and hills
and gather stones to build as high
as my new kind of balance will permit.
A little lopsided, inept as yet
in my new frame of thinking,
I walk this old familiar path
drunk on dustlessness, aslant to every norm.
And yet I feel, as I move strangely on,
weaving through the world and dreams,
that God whistles in the branches all around me
and scatters stones for me to find while walking
and builds the hills of dust,
roots the trees in mud,
to hint to me where life might really stand
on this issue of spring cleaning.

A Different Kind of Love

Some passions may amuse,
like mine for words.
In words my separate selves
begin to fuse
and find their singular expression–
strange confession–
though neither time nor words suffice
to capture all.

Time mellows us a little,
letting us from narrow confines reach;
but perfect words can teach
us what we are about.

Out from insensibility we rise,
whether or not our words are wise.
They teach us who we are
and how we see the world
and make concrete our values
that we might never realize
or find a way to show.

Sometimes it's not enough to see
or hear or feel or even touch.
A little, a lot, however much,
sometimes we have to tell ourselves
just what we know.

Hiding

I have known the need to hide.
Dark fears may come unbidden
to live at a child's side
that leave her terrified
of the world's unkindness.

I have known the need to stop hiding.
Deep joys, never anticipated,
await the soul
who becomes whole,
emancipated.

It isn't one way or the other;
both paths may co-exist.
I would resist the invitation
to live always in the open
and as strongly the temptation
to hide again in silence.
But here and there within the grass

or camouflaged in dust or air,
some fragment lingers hoping
that no gathering hand will find it,
no starbeams light it into view,
no nightmare find it in its sleep,
while, too, that some beloved mind,
heart, ear, will sometimes hear it
and respond
and care.

Patterns

I flicker with the shifting light,
patterns of sky all flecked with snow,

sensing patterns in the random fall
of stars and men and trees that grow
in unknown places.

I see the changing patterns
and the scattered rich designs

of stray actions finding value
in time's infinite mines
of possibility.
I am an awkward pendulum,
shifting in a stiff, erratic way,

halting briefly now at order,
then at chaos where I mostly stay,
accumulating wonder.

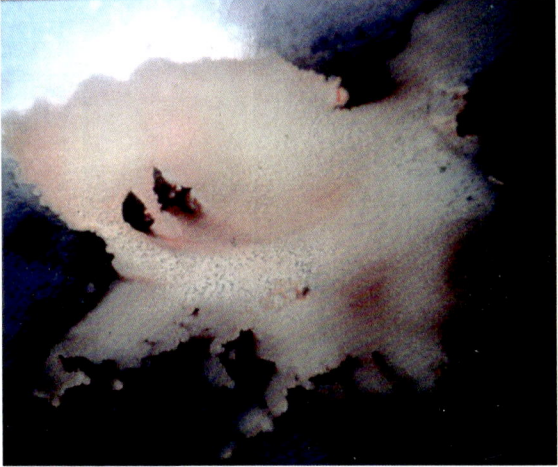

PLATE I

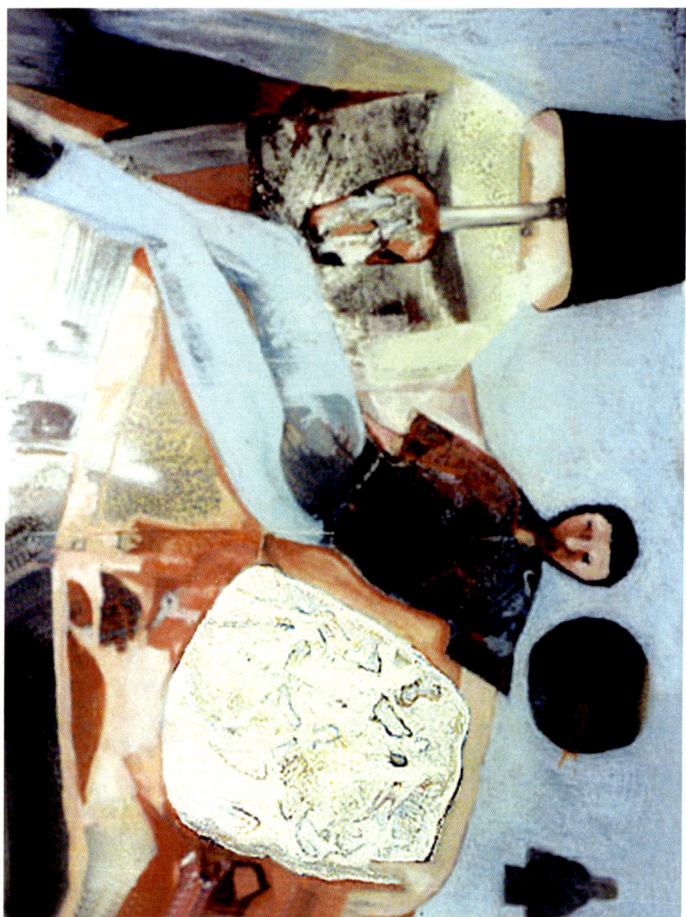

PLATE II

PLATE III

PLATE IV

PLATE V

PLATE VI

PLATE VII

In a Ghostly Sculpture Garden
©1999, mdbrown

PLATE VIII

Resident of Ghost Town

He sits apart
on a whitening slope,
alone and trackless in surreal snow

to watch the drifts
encompass frail gray structures,
surrounding each
in coats of deadly white.

Ghost town, mood town. . .
waiting for the whistle
of a train, of a bird
to bring back life.

No tracks, no ties, no whistles.
The trains soar beyond the distant slopes;
the birds get de-railed;
the pale drifts billow
like ghosts of spirit snow,
sinking fragile sculptures
in coats of deadly white.

Caving

I explored the dark recesses
of one black onyx cave
where anger gathered its accretions,
refusing to dissolve,
and built its crusted pillars
for the future.

How, except with love

and with warm good will,
does one combat the sediments
of anger?
With gentle ways
one softens the effects
which, left alone,
would stretch to eons
each taut day.

Sometimes a cave does not admit
a gentle path;
it will not fill with love,
insisting that it must be hollow,
by definition empty
but for its free-formed croppings
of cold stone.

Then we are all caved in,
immobilized by intellect
and by a pillared will
against the soft dissolving nature
of a flow of tears.

I would flood this cave
if I knew how,
and I would change the nature
of these pillars
to towers of strength
that knew when crumbling was a virtue.
I'd like to see the bleak and narrow corridors
glow with a new-found feeling
and widen out to unexpected pools.

Then good-by to caves–
no more constructed barriers of stone
all intricately carved to hide
their true resources,

no more vaults of darkness
to lock out warmth
and light.

August Dusk

This hour seems meant for play:
the children stretch the sun far into night,
but leafy smells and magic spells surround
the trees. Each blossom features
haloes of indifferent power. Time
slides infinitely lazy
along each bough.
Dusk comes so mellow now
in summer's prime.
The little winged and knotty creatures
gather on a slender ledge of sound
to breathe the final light
of every day.

On into dark to outlast the sun
the crickets sing the children dreamward-bound.
The tendrils of this hour,
which spiral invisibly through the dark mind,
wind not to future power
but into far more fertile ground
before they're done.

Childhood Nights

Spiders used to crawl
above the closet door,
across the wall,
or so it looked to me.
They were merely shadows,
though I never knew of what.
Mesmerized, I'd stare
at long dark fingers stretching there
or pull the covers higher over head
but be afraid to sleep,
never knowing what might choose
to creep upon the bed.

The coiled radiator
nightly hissed,
snakelike, in the winter cold.
Reflections from the lights of cars
raced around the ceilings, bold
in their eerie speed.
I never missed
the snake or spiders later
when, old enough to think them through,
I was freed.

But there were other things as well,
that to a child turn the night
into a major kind of hell:
towers of blocks would slowly build
in silence
but then that silence filled the room,
and then the blocks would crash
in depths of quiet that pierced the ears,
making them go numb.
Dragons unfolded in the corners,
breathing fire from yawning mouths,

their teeth aching to eat human flesh.
Sleep shivered in the covers
and daylight came too soon, too late.
The mind is not refreshed.

We think we send our children
safely to their beds,
never contemplating images
that might invade their heads,
incur their fearful sleeplessness,
destroy their childhood happiness.
We tell them they are safe because we're there;
but so are shadow spiders, snakes,
eerie lights, fire-breathing dragon frights,
and other waking nightmares in the air.

Late Autumn

It is that time of year
when all the orange and the gold
that filled the trees
have faded down to gray and brown.
The flocks of geese in standard vees
join forces over the smoky land,
circling once, then fleeing cold.

It used to be a time of year
when sadness fell in sleeting rain,
or snow in sooty flakes came down.
Life seemed a dull monotony:
I circled then but did not flee–
no need like geese to find another place
if all would stay the same.

Now autumn with no change of name
wears a different shape and face,
descends with a poignant kind of grace
that seems harmonious, not dull.
It brings a sense of fullness
before deep winter ice begins.
And even then, when life is in deep freeze,
I look out on the barest trees
that house the creatures who stay in place
to find what the season stores.

In Wyoming

In Wyoming the wind
shoots from the hip
and gusts in large upreaching curves
across the rocks
to brush the dust in wideflung sweeps
over the chapped and bristled land.
Cowboy history and records of Earth
meet on the highways and the plains;
deer with their fawns nibble and graze
along the thin running fences,
under the low and ranging clouds.
Haunting the shadows are tribal legends,
hiding in cliffs and in hills.

And all this open space is new to me.
Slowly the words will filter in
to accommodate new perceptions.

The austere plains give way to Yellowstone,
sulphur and rust and deep pine green
and everywhere havens for eyes..

I am pulled silent to these bright canyons,
drawn by their strong stone rhythms
and by their visual power
to solitary wandering
here on their high trails.
Clear waters rush and rumble through the rocks,
roaring and hissing to the canyon floor,
and yet it seems so hushed, so voiceless here.
The hawks and gulls, the jays that call,
blend in the wealthy meadow of sound,
a silence rich in acceptable paradox.

Words always work a magic on my mind
but not like mountains
which fill the ample sky with healing power
and soothe the ragged peaks of discontent
for just as long as they remain
hoarded behind my eyes.

                    *

The sun floats down
and tall grass and scrub
yield a larger treasure of game:
moose and elk and buffalo
drift through the valleys and disappear.
It is a lonely world,
despite the abundance of life that roams,
visible or not, its many trails.
In this transient moment I am here
with eyes reluctant even to blink
lest they miss the flicker of some brief life
behind a flower or blade of grass.
And I am aware that I, too, drift
toward disappearances of my own
and that all that keep these scenes alive
are eyes and slow-filtering words.

On Hanging a New Feeder

Squirrels and raccoons destroyed them all,
chewing the cords that tied them to the trees,
letting the feeders fall
and, being plastic, break
at the first strong breeze.
This time I got a wooden box
to hold the suet blocks.
I hung it where no sane raccoon
would seek a place to test its weight,
no agile squirrel create a private plate
of seed or fat to sate its appetite.

Too many bullies have I known
who have no need to oust the smaller birds,
though they exert their power.
The doves for all their dim IQ,
have learned to accept their lowly fate
and let the larger critters feed
while they just strut a bit and wait
for manna falling from a few feet up,
hoping for some to fill their cup.

All my politics show through,
whether in small deeds or words:
I feed the ones who cannot push or shove,
the ones unable to make their move,
who meekly settle for meager crumbs.
I'd like to see a revolution
wherein the bullies are overthrown,
leading to widespread evolution
and to a future now unknown.

Touching the Stars

I dreamed of a large darkened hall
and I alone within.
Somewhere beyond the farthest wall
a wedding was going on.
I was alone in the room,
far from the bride and the groom.

The floor was a glossy wood,
gleaming as if brand new,
reflecting a light at the door,
and I was waiting for You.
No one came through.

Dimly I started to see,
hanging huge on every black wall
the covers of all of my books,
named yet or not,
written or not,
framed and standing tall.
I could walk into them.
Where were You?

A hole opened up in the floor,
but really something greater:
a sea of stars, a cosmic pool,
a crater of light for me alone.

I dipped my feet in the stars
and touched all with my hand,
and the dream hung there suspended;
but after the vision ended,
my eyes still shone.

Now I touch the stars in the rippled sky,
knowing I am not real,

that at my soaring, I dissolve,
falling again to the dark.

I reach to the stars in the reflecting sea,
knowing they are not real,
that at my touch
all light dissolves,
dispersing again to the dark.

I touch the stars that light my eyes,
eclipsing all in my act,
blinding myself by the deed;
but then from darkness and from pain
I may grow real,
whole again,
wherever You are.

Long Time Passes

Long has it been
since our summer days
dwelled in the branches of apple trees,
lingered in meadows dappled bright
with blossoms playing host to bees,
and the sun brought comfort
to our well-loved old.

No more, for they have not stayed to play.
Too few picnics out on the lawn
with croquet and badminton going on;
too few family left to share
the bees and the birds and the blue, blue air.

Taken from us like honey from trees,
with no apology or if you please,

. . . to a better world?

One by one we are brought to our knees,
made to see that our victories
might just as well have stayed close-curled
in cocoons of their pre-imaginings.
Long has it been since we were assured
of a waiting sphere in the cosmic seas,
. . . a world of joy for the chosen few?

What if not me? What if not you?

Slowly we have become inured
to the loss of human eternities.
And yet heart clings to a human hope
and a simple faith in human dreams
that life is much more than it seems
and far less cold.

Small Songs

I don't pretend to be content
with messages too large for me.
Sing all you want in gigantic tunes
of one true love eternally–
blind or deaf I'll be.

Don't sing of a god who loves all alike
(but your friends a little more)
or the angel who rescues one burning life,
while skipping a thousand and four.
Those aren't the songs I'll keep.

But lyrics wrapped
in yellow leaves

or tapped in code on window panes
that croon through rains to cool our griefs
and soften the pounding thunder–
these speak to me.
Under their spell I'll calmly sleep
and dream of a god I comprehend,
one who comprehends me.

The Wood-Bearers

Book in hand, I sat on the grass,
shaded by the sweet gum tree,
peacefully napping,
when a gentle lapping of another time
and a scent of mystery from an older place,
shook through my mind, surrounding self.
There in the side of the green slope nearby,
earth opened up dream's grounded space;
and a weathered wood door appeared,
slowly creaking open. I rubbed each eye.
Out from within, like immense balloons
twisting with every breeze,
three giant figures floated,
solemn and coated in silence,
larger than full-grown trees.
Each wore a leather tunic,
sported a medieval cap;
each bore a hundred great timbers
chained to his muscular back.
Burdened, they flew toward heaven.
Wood dust sprinkled like rain.
I thought, *what a strange nap!*

Like Alice on finding the rabbit hole,

I peered into the darkness beyond the door.
In I crawled down a passage
too narrow for me,
let alone for a giant woodman,
still more so even for three.
I emerged on a stone balcony
that looked down to a circular room
whose ceiling rose to a massive height.
From my place on a kind of mezzanine,
I gazed down on a veined marble floor.
The only soul was one monk in white
leaving through a modern glass door.

I feared I'd encroached on a sacred scene;
but down the stone stairs I went,
carefully, slowly, somewhat afraid,
alone in that large stone hall
still holding mystery's scent
but otherwise bare
except for the floor, the circular wall,
and the door's bright glare.

An alcove appeared on the right,
looking at first like a tomb
lit dimly by candlelight:
an altar, two tapers, a place meant for prayer.
Wordless I knelt a long time there,
knowing nothing of mass;
but a part of me prayed to understand
while the rest of me slept in the grass.

True Romance

What if the world fails to survive
all the bickerings of grown-up boys

who think that it was meant for them?

I see the trees in their thin winter stands,
shivering in the winds of icy war
until red blood ignites and flows
deep into earth.

Hatred will thrive
on all our tinkering with local toys
that quickly create worldwide mayhem
and devour the woods and the flowering lands,
taking us all from where we are
into a region none of us knows
deep in the red-soaked earth.

I watch the birds that still fly free,
briefly escaping gravity
and darkly human hostility.

Truest romance is with life itself
and love of the world in its native state.
It turns its face away from hate
and deepens its love of Earth.

One Scatter of Snow

One scatter of snow
and someone somewhere glows
while elsewhere another dies
of cold.

How can we think we know
that whatever of truth shows
up for us is not, for another, lies?
As we grow old

and the scatter of snow
lightens our once-dark hair,
life seems more fragile everywhere
and truth too complex to know,
no matter how simple.

Convincing

He convinced her that she was lazy.
Scarcely a word was needed,
for how could she think otherwise
when tumbleweeds collected in corners,
dishes meandered to the kitchen sink?
She didn't pause to think
how odd it was that she should grow most tense
deprived of action,
that only immersed in doing
did she feel alive.
She took as true
the badgering forever,
her effort too little, overdue,
as if the only present
she was allowed to give
was absolute denial
of self, of need, and of desire.
Why live for anything other than him?
All things were wrong,
excess or insufficient fire,
nothing ever in the middle,
nothing right.
No satisfaction for jobs done.

More and more she learned
what mattered most,

what kept her soul from feeling lost,
her mind not a pale ghost
of what it might have been.

In all those things
he played no part.
She thought of marriage as a kind of dance,
the art of sharing a difficult balance
to create a caring place
where each was a willing anchor for the other.

He convinced her that she was worthless,
not good enough for him, so far above;
so when she finally convinced herself
that he required too much work,
it wasn't because of laziness
but because of the death of love.

Ella

Poor little Ella,
chained to a broom,
sweeping ashes.
Sad little Ella,
confined to a room
too small for her
while just on the other side of the wall
in magnificent sashes
perhaps is the prince who will sweep her away
to a vast palatial hall,
except that he does not know of her yet
or her existence.
She dreams at first of a fancy ball
at which she shines, astonishing all.
But always a deeper part of her knows

that a room of grandeur of any size
is no less confining,
has no more of grace
unless she is free to be who she is
and to grow.

She will not be bought
by a saviour prince
eager to marry,
briefly entranced by her beauty.
His white steed will carry
some other maid
as she flees from the thought
of chains of all kinds
and escapes to a higher duty:
adulthood.

Let Cinderella of fantasy
find happiness ever after
in shoes of glass
and the prince's hand
that leads her to bed as her glory
where she will produce a fine heir.

It may be a marvelous fairy tale
or may be a dismal story,
but that life is not for our heroine;
our Ella is not there.